Look What You Can Make With

Plastic-Foam
Trays

Edited by Kelly Milner Halls

Boyds Mills Press

Craft Coordinator:

Kelly Milner Halls

Craft Makers:

Rebecca Ent
Kelly Milner Halls
Kerry O'Neill

Contributors:

Patricia Barley
Katherine Corliss Bartow
Barbara Bell
Carol Borowsky
Doris D. Breiholz
June Budd
Barbara Casper
Donna Collinsworth
Kent Douglas
Paige Eckard
Clara Flammang

Nancy H. Giles
Anne Gray
Leslie Hamilton
Texie Hering
Ann Lewandowski
Lee Lindeman
Teresa Matichka
Kerry O'Neill
Helen M. Pedersen
James Perrin
Jane K. Priewe

Kathy Ross
Helen Sattler
Mary Shea
Andrew J. Smith
Cheryl Stees
June Swanson
Bea Talson
Sharon Dunn Umnik
Jean Wood

Copyright © 2003 by Boyds Mills Press
All rights reserved

Published by Bell Books
Boyds Mills Press, Inc.
A Highlights Company
815 Church Street
Honesdale, Pennsylvania 18431
Printed in China

Publisher Cataloging-in-Publication Data (U.S.)

Look what you can make with plastic-foam trays : over 90 pictured crafts
and dozens of other ideas / edited by Kelly Milner Halls.—1st ed.
[48] p. : col. photos. ;   cm.
Includes index.
Summary: Toys, games, and other things to make from plastic-foam trays.
ISBN 1-59078-078-7
1. Handicrafts—Juvenile literature. 2. Plastics craft—Juvenile
literature. 3. Toy making—Juvenile literature. I. Halls, Kelly Milner.
II. Title.
745.5/ 72 21   2003
2002109581

First edition, 2003
Books in this series originally designed by Lorianne Siomades
The text of this book is set in 10-point Avant Garde Demi, titles 43-point Gill Sans Extra Bold.

Photographs by Earl & Sedor Photographic

Visit our Web site at www.boydsmillspress.com

10 9 8 7 6 5 4 3 2 1

Getting Started

his book is filled with fun, easy-to-make crafts, and each one begins with a plastic-foam tray. You'll ind a wide variety of things to make, including toys, games, and gifts.

Directions

3efore you start each craft, read he directions and look closely at the photograph, but emember—it's up to you to make the craft your own. If we decorate a craft with markers out you want to use glitter paint and stickers, go for it. Feel free o stray from our directions and nvent new crafts.

Work Area

t's a good idea to keep your work area covered. Old newspapers, brown paper (from grocery bags), or old sheets work well. Also, protect your clothes by wearing a smock. A big old shirt does the job and gives you room to move. Finally, emember to clean up when you've finished.

Materials

You'll need plastic-foam trays, so start saving now. Ask friends and relatives to help. Make sure your foam trays are washed with soap and dried before you use them. You might want to use a table knife to cut shapes from your plastic foam. If necessary, smooth the edges with fine sandpaper. Craft glue is the best type of glue to use on plastic foam. Let the glue dry overnight.

To add color to plastic foam, we recommend using permanent markers or acrylic paint. Keep your craft-making supplies together, and before making each craft, check the "You Will Need" list to make sure you have everything. Also, since you'll need scissors, craft glue, tape, or a stapler for almost every craft, we don't list these supplies.

Other Stuff

When we show several similar crafts, we'll often list numbered directions that apply to all of the crafts, then specific directions for each craft. Plus, you'll find other ways to jazz up your projects in the "More Ideas" section that appears with every craft. You'll also think of new ideas of your own once you get rolling. So browse through these pages, choose a craft, and have some creative fun. Before you know it, you'll be showing everyone what you made with plastic-foam trays.

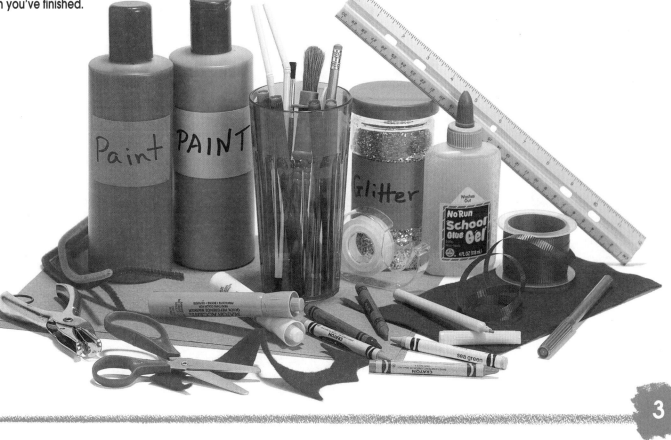

My Bulletin Board

Keep your special reminders handy on these cheerful boards.

To Make the Mini Bulletin Board

Glue a rectangle of felt to the inside bottom of the foam tray. Glue pompoms around the felt edges. Pick out pasta letters to spell whatever message you would like on your bulletin board. Glue in place. Decorate the bottom corners of the board with foam animals or pictures from magazines. Add a ribbon hanger to the top.

To Make the Memo Board

Attach a small calendar and message pads to a foam tray with craft glue. Cut a curved edge from a foam tray, and glue in place for a pencil tray. Poke two holes in the top, and add a ribbon or yarn hanger.

To Make the Fabric-Squares Board

Arrange foam rectangles on a large piece of cardboard. Make a sketch of the arrangement on paper to help you remember where the rectangles go. Lay each rectangle on a large piece of fabric. Spread glue on two opposite sides of each rectangle. Fold the fabric over the edges into the glue. Hold with clothespins until dry. Then glue the other two sides. Paint the cardboard. Let dry. Glue the fabric-covered rectangles onto the cardboard. Add a ribbon hanger if you wish.

To Make the Fabric Board

Poke two holes at the top of a large foam tray, and add ribbon or yarn for a hanger. Glue a piece of fabric over the tray. Add a felt flower and letters.

More Ideas

Make an extra-large bulletin board by binding four of the small boards together at the corners using a hole punch and yarn or ribbon.

Foam-Fish Bowl

You don't need to feed these guppies.

You Will Need:

- small plastic-foam tray
- permanent markers
- sewing needle
- thread
- rustproof screws or nuts
- clear jar with lid
- sand or aquarium gravel
- water

1 Draw two small fish on a plastic-foam tray. Decorate with markers.

2 Cut the fish from the tray.

3 Using a sewing needle, attach a length of thread to each of the foam fish at the belly. Tie the loose end of the thread to a small screw or nut.

4 Drop the fish and tether into a clean jar with a secure lid. Add a layer of sand or aquarium gravel to cover the screws or nuts.

5 Carefully fill the jar with water. Screw the lid on and set the "aquarium" on a shelf.

More Ideas

Add a drop of blue food coloring to the water to make it look like seawater.

Cut-It-Up Puzzle

Piece together this make-it-yourself jigsaw.

You Will Need:

- small plastic-foam tray
- magazine picture
- marker or pencil
- plastic bag

1 Cut the curved sides off a plastic-foam tray.

2 Glue a magazine picture to the flat part of the tray.

3 Turn the foam over. Using a marker or pencil, draw lines on the back to create different sections.

4 Cut the puzzle into pieces, following the lines you made on the back.

5 Store your puzzle pieces in a plastic bag.

More Ideas

Draw your own picture on the plastic foam and cut it out. Give to a friend to put together.

Tabletop Weather Vanes

Decorate your room with these colorful birds.

You Will Need:

- plastic-foam trays
- metal paper fasteners
- pen
- clean pudding cups
- chenille sticks

1 For each weather vane, cut the shape of a bird from a plastic-foam tray. Cut two wings from the tray.

2 Fasten the wings to the body with a paper fastener. Draw an eye with a pen.

3 Poke a hole in the bottom of a pudding cup.

4 Tape one end of the chenille stick to the back of the bird. Place the cup upside down. Push the other end of the stick into the hole.

More Ideas

Instead of birds, make a cow, chicken, or other animal shape you might find on outdoor weather vanes.

Greetings for the Seasons

Wish your friends and relatives a happy holiday.

You Will Need:

- construction paper or poster board
- plastic-foam trays
- permanent markers
- rhinestones and other trims
- hole punch
- gold paint and paintbrush

To Make the Thanksgiving Card

Glue construction-paper feathers to the card, then add a turkey shape on top.

To Make the Valentine's Day Card

Punch holes in foam-tray scraps and glue the dots to a heart shape.

To Make the Basic Card

1 Fold a piece of construction paper or poster board to make a greeting card.

2 Cut out holiday shapes from foam trays, and decorate with markers and trims.

3 Add your message inside the card.

Happy Thanksgiving!

Happy Valentine's Day!

To Make the Yom Kippur Card

Cut a *shofar* (ram's horn) from a plastic-foam tray and decorate. Make Stars of David from construction paper. Glue the shapes to the card.

To Make the Hanukkah Card

Cut a menorah from a plastic-foam tray, paint it gold, and glue it to the card.

To Make the Christmas Card

Add rhinestone ornaments to the branches.

More Ideas

For St. Patrick's Day, glue shamrock shapes around the card.

Foam-Disk Wigglers

Wiggle and giggle with these foam-made creatures.

You Will Need:

- plastic-foam trays
- sewing needle
- thread
- craft beads
- chenille sticks
- plastic wiggle eyes
- rhinestones

To Make the Basic Wiggler

1 Cut circles from plastic-foam trays.

2 With a needle and thread, slide the circles onto the thread.

3 Add a small bead in between the circles.

4 When you are finished, knot the thread so the disks stay tight.

To Make the Bee

Add some large yellow circles in with black circles. Shape a chenille stick into wings, and wind it around the body. Shape a chenille stick piece into a V. Curve the ends to make antennae. Stick the bottom into the edge of the first circle. Add plastic wiggle eyes.

To Make the Worm

Draw circles about the size of a half-dollar over the flat part of a plastic-foam tray. Cut them out. Cut two circles to the size of dimes, and cut four circles to the size of nickels. Slide the foam disks onto the thread, starting with one of the dime-sized disks, then two of the nickel disks, then all of the half-dollar-sized disks. Thread a small bead between each disk. Add the last two nickel-sized disks and the last dime-sized circle with a bead between each one. Knot the thread. Glue plastic wiggle eyes and a rhinestone to one end of the worm.

To Make the Ant

Make small black plastic-foam circles. Attach pieces of chenille stick to the body as legs. Add a funny-shaped head from plastic foam.

More Ideas

Make a woolly bear caterpillar with black and brown circles.

Nifty Nameplates

Tell the world who you are.

You Will Need:

- small plastic-foam trays
- construction paper
- permanent markers
- glitter
- ribbon
- sequins or buttons

1 Cut a plastic-foam tray to the size you want, leaving a flat surface.

2 Cut a piece of construction paper just slightly smaller than your foam piece.

3 Write your name on the paper using bright colors and glitter.

4 Glue the construction paper to the foam piece.

5 Glue a ribbon border around the plate. Decorate the corners with sequins or tiny buttons. Add a ribbon hanger to the back.

More Ideas

Make a nameplate for your hamster's cage or your dog's house. Decorate with construction-paper bones or paw prints.

Little Chicken

Hang this barnyard favorite in your kitchen.

You Will Need:

- large plastic-foam tray
- permanent markers
- yarn

1 Draw the shape of a chicken, a wing, and four small eggs on your plastic-foam tray. Cut them out.

2 Decorate them with markers.

3 Glue the eggs to two 4-inch lengths of yarn. Glue the yarn to the back of the chicken.

4 Glue a yarn hanger to the top of the chicken.

More Ideas

Is red your color? Draw cardinals instead of chickens for a colorful alternative. Yellow? How about canaries? Blue? Bluebirds. Black? Think crows.

Christmas Cutouts

These light and festive ornaments will brighten your holidays.

You Will Need:

- plastic-foam trays
- permanent markers
- glitter
- hole punch
- ribbon
- sewing needle
- metallic thread

1 Draw your favorite holiday shape on a plastic-foam tray. Cut it out.

2 Decorate with markers, glitter, and whatever else you'd like to use.

3 Punch a hole in the top of the ornament.

4 Thread a piece of satin ribbon through the hole. Or with a sewing needle, attach metallic thread to the ornament. Knot the ends.

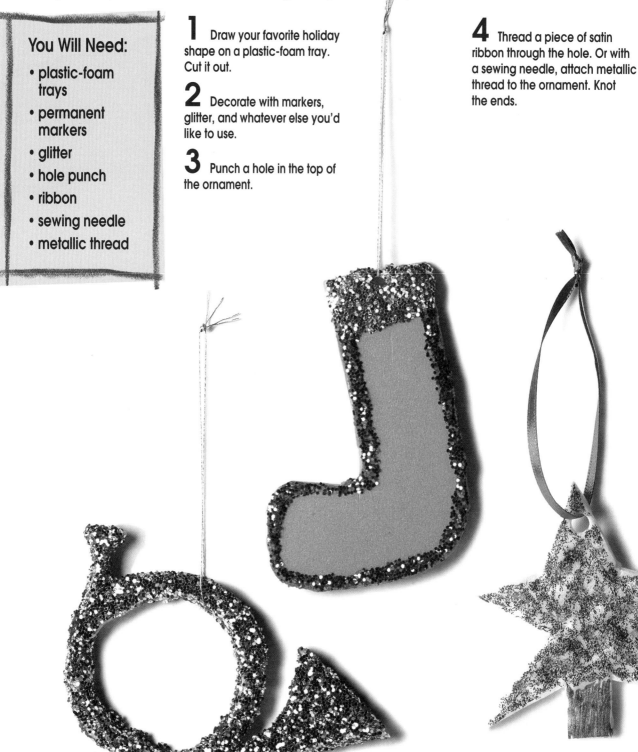

More Ideas

Get creative with your shapes and designs. Stars, candy canes, and angels are only a few of the possibilities. Love cartoons? Have a cartoon-character Christmas with plastic foam, glue, and magazine cutouts.

Coupon Catcher

File those money-saving coupons in one safe place.

You Will Need:

- two small plastic-foam trays
- hole punch
- permanent markers
- glitter
- chenille sticks or yarn

1 Cut a plastic-foam tray in half. Set the second half aside.

2 Punch holes in the curved edges of the half tray and the lower half of the whole tray.

3 With markers, write *Coupons* on the bottom of the half tray. Decorate with glitter.

4 Fit the two trays together to form a pocket, and lace together with chenille sticks or yarn.

5 Add a hanger to the top.

More Ideas

String two or three catchers together to make a handy filing system.

Bits-and-Pieces Mosaic

Piece together this work of art.

You Will Need:

- different-colored plastic-foam trays
- pencil or marker

1 Cut the curved edges off a plastic-foam tray.

2 Draw a large, simple design on the flat part of the foam tray.

3 Cut small, odd-shaped pieces from other foam trays.

4 Fill in the outlines with the cut pieces, gluing them in place.

More Ideas

Create nameplates as shown on page 11, but do it in this mosaic style.

Wacky Masks

Make a mask to suit your mood.

You Will Need:

- plastic-foam trays
- crayons
- construction paper
- yarn
- hole punch
- snow glitter
- rhinestones and other trims
- two craft sticks

To Make the Clown Mask

Add features from construction paper. Glue on yarn hair. Punch a hole in each side of the mask, and tie yarn through the holes.

To Make the Cat Mask

Cover the mask shape with black construction paper. Then mark and cut out the eyeholes. Add cut-paper features. Draw on whiskers. Punch a hole in each side of the mask, and tie yarn through the holes.

To Make the Snow Mask

Smooth a thick layer of craft glue over the mask. Add a thick layer of snow glitter on top. Decorate with rhinestones and other trims. Glue two craft sticks together. Let dry. Glue the combined sticks to the side of the mask.

More Ideas

Replace the white glitter with a brighter color. Add craft feathers or chenille sticks.

A black bat mask could be fun to make with glitter and sequins in dark colors.

To Make the Basic Mask

1. Draw a mask shape on the flat surface of a plastic-foam tray and cut it out.

2. Hold the mask up to your face and mark the eyeholes with a crayon.

3. Take off the mask and cut out the eyeholes.

Mobile Magic

Dangle these colorful hang-ups so everyone can see them.

You Will Need:

- plastic-foam trays
- sewing needle
- embroidery or metallic thread
- clear fishing line
- permanent markers
- glitter
- plastic wiggle eyes
- metal paper fasteners
- craft beads
- small plastic ring

To Make the Shamrock Mobile

Color the shamrock shapes front and back with green marker. Add glitter and plastic wiggle eyes.

To Make the Sunshine Mobile

Cut sun, star, and crescent moon shapes. Add features with glitter and marker.

To Make the Basic Mobile

1 Draw shapes on a plastic-foam tray and cut them out. Cut out a triangle shape from the foam for a base.

2 Thread a needle with thread or fishing line and knot the end. Using the needle, poke a hole through the top of each shape. Attach the other end of the thread through one corner of the triangle. Knot the end.

3 Add a thread hanger.

To Make the Bird Mobile

Cut bird and wing shapes. Attach two wings on opposite sides of the bird with a paper fastener. Use fishing line to attach the birds to the triangle base. Gather up the three lines and add beads. Tie the end of the line to a ring for a hanger.

To Make the Butterfly Mobile

Outline the butterfly shapes with glitter. Use metallic thread to hang the shapes.

More Ideas

Change the shape and color to suit the holiday. Cut out eggs for Easter, stars for Christmas, candles for Hanukkah, pumpkins for Halloween.

Beads and Bangles Jewelry

Make a fashion statement.

You Will Need:

- heavy thread
- plastic-foam trays
- sewing needle
- craft beads
- glitter, sequins, and other trims

To Make the Basic Jewelry

1 Cut heavy thread to the length you want. Knot the end.

2 Cut out small shapes from plastic foam.

3 Using a sewing needle, string beads and foam pieces onto the thread.

To Make the Heart Necklace

Cut a heart shape from plastic foam, and decorate with glitter and other trims. Sew through the center of each plastic-foam shape, adding cylinder beads as you go. Sew the ends of the thread through the foam heart. Knot each end.

To Make the Bracelets

Cut a length of thread that will go around the palm of your hand. Knot the end. String the beads and foam shapes onto the thread. Knot the ends together.

More Ideas

Make this jewelry for your mom or grandmother to give to her on Mother's Day.

Something's Fishy Aquarium

This fish will never need feeding while you're on vacation.

You Will Need:

- construction paper
- markers
- small plastic-foam tray
- colored plastic wrap

1 Cut out underwater shapes from construction paper. Decorate them with markers.

2 Glue them to the flat part of a plastic-foam tray.

3 Cover the tray with colored plastic wrap.

More Ideas

Glue small three-dimensional objects to your aquarium, such as fake coral or a plastic diver. You can find these items at a tropical fish store or discount store.

Shield of Honor

Make your own official crest.

You Will Need:

- large plastic-foam tray
- construction paper

1 Cut a shield shape from a large plastic-foam tray.

2 Glue on narrow strips of construction paper to create sections on the shield.

3 Cut out shapes from paper that represent who you are and what you like. Add your initials in cut paper.

More Ideas

Cover part of the shield with aluminum foil for a metallic effect.

Animal Foam Faces

These friends will hang around for years.

You Will Need:

- plastic-foam trays
- felt
- plastic wiggle eyes
- yarn
- marker or pen
- straw
- ribbon
- pink crayon

To Make the Lion

Draw features on light brown felt with marker. Glue pieces of straw around the edge of the face for a mane. Add a ribbon bow at the neck.

To Make the Bear

Glue a pink felt tongue under the large brown nose. Glue white felt circles under the eyes.

To Make the Cat

Cut two small gray felt circles to form the cat's snout. Glue a pink triangle of felt over the circles and a pink circle of felt under them to form the nose and mouth.

To Make the Monkey

Cut a monkey face from light brown felt and glue it on top of a dark brown circle. Add felt ears and other features. Draw on a mouth.

To Make the Basic Face

1 Cut a circle from a plastic-foam tray.

2 Cut the same-sized circle of felt, and glue it to the plastic-foam circle.

3 Cut features from felt and glue in place.

4 Add two plastic wiggle eyes or felt eyes.

5 Add a yarn hanger to the back.

To Make the Rabbit

Cut long white ear shapes and glue them to the top of the circle. Add a bow in between the ears. Smudge a little pink crayon on the rabbit's cheeks.

More Ideas

Make a mobile out of your favorite animal faces. How about creatures no one's ever seen?

Garden Markers

Time for your family to plant vegetables? These markers will tell you what's what.

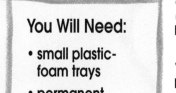

You Will Need:

- small plastic-foam trays
- permanent markers
- craft sticks

1 Cut away the curved part of the trays, leaving the flat parts. Cut these in half.

2 Cut a slit near the top and bottom of each flat piece.

3 On the foam, draw a picture of each vegetable you will plant.

4 Insert a craft stick through the slits.

More Ideas

Make markers for your flower garden so you'll know which blooms are about to take root.

Nest of Chicks

Dress up your springtime table with these foam fluffs.

You Will Need:

- plastic-foam trays
- permanent markers
- ribbon
- Easter grass

1 Cut three chicks from plastic-foam trays.

2 Decorate with marker and ribbon.

3 Turn another tray over so the bottom faces up. Cut three slits, each large enough to fit one chick.

4 Spread a thick layer of glue across the foam tray. Add Easter grass on top. Let dry completely.

5 Place each chick in a slit. Brush glue around the chicks underneath the tray.

More Ideas

If your foam tray is extra-large, arrange real colored Easter eggs in with the foam chicks for a special effect.

Stained-Glass Tissue Window

Let the colors shine through this beautiful foam project.

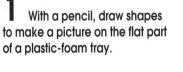

You Will Need:

- pencil
- plastic-foam tray
- colored tissue paper
- glitter or other trims

1 With a pencil, draw shapes to make a picture on the flat part of a plastic-foam tray.

2 Carefully cut the shapes out of the foam tray.

3 Cut pieces of colored tissue paper.

4 Cover the cut shapes with the tissue pieces, gluing them on the back of the foam tray. Let dry.

5 Add an outline of glitter around the shapes if you wish.

More Ideas

Use this basic idea to create other translucent pictures. Tropical fish and geometric designs work especially well.

Festive Foam Hang-Ups

Make these ornaments for all the holidays throughout the year.

You Will Need:

- large and small plastic-foam trays
- permanent markers
- sewing needle
- metallic or embroidery thread
- glitter
- hole punch
- paint and paintbrush
- ruler

To Make the Ghost

Cut a ghost shape from a foam tray. Outline the shape with black marker. Add features. Poke a hole at the top with a needle and add a thread hanger.

To Make the Valentine's Day Heart

Cut a heart shape from a pink foam tray. Outline with glitter. Draw a smaller glitter heart in the center. Use a hole punch to make a hole at the top. Add a metallic-thread hanger.

To Make the Easter Egg

Cut an egg shape from a foam tray. Paint the foam tan. To make the designs, brush on several layers of paint until the patterns are raised. Let dry thoroughly. Poke a hole at the top with a hole punch. Add a thread hanger.

To Make the Flag

Cut a flag shape from a large plastic-foam tray. Measure a square in the left-hand corner and twelve horizontal lines. Color the flag with markers. Add glitter for stars. Poke a hole at the top with a needle and add metallic thread. Knot the ends of the thread to make a hanger.

To Make the Star of David

Cut a Star of David shape from a foam tray. Color with marker. Use a hole punch to make a hole at the top. Add metallic thread for a hanger.

More Ideas

Make several ornaments for a holiday, and tie them to a length of ribbon. Tie the garland to a curtain rod on a window. (Ask permission first.)

Medieval Castle

Rejoice, knights and ladies, and celebrate a splendid home.

You Will Need:

- two large plastic-foam trays
- pencil
- black permanent marker
- toothpicks
- thread

1 Cut off the short sides of each tray, leaving the long curved sides uncut. Then cut the long sides in half lengthwise.

2 With scissors, snip every ½ inch along the curved edges. Bend every other tab created by the slits. Snap the tabs off.

3 Use a pencil point to carve out windows and a drawbridge. Tape the walls together at the corners, inside and out.

4 Outline the windows with black marker. Draw bricks on the front.

5 Stick foam flags on toothpicks and insert them into the castle. Tape thread to the drawbridge and the inside of the castle.

More Ideas

Make miniature shields from paper and hang them over the castle walls.

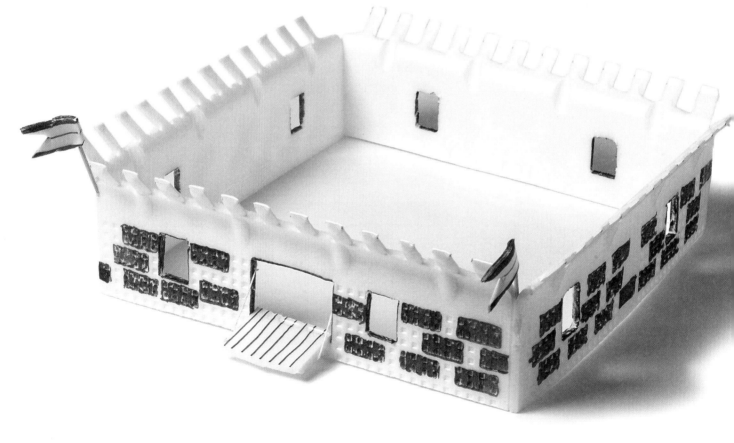

Napkin Pocket

Make this the center of your breakfast table.

You Will Need:

- three plastic-foam trays
- heavy cardboard
- paint and paintbrush
- construction paper

1 Cut three plastic-foam trays in half.

2 Glue two halves together, forming a pocket. Do the same for the other trays. Let dry.

3 Glue the three pockets side by side. Let dry. Then glue the bottoms to the cardboard.

4 Paint the holder and cardboard base. Let dry.

5 Add cut-paper decorations to both sides of the holder.

More Ideas

Instead of construction paper, use felt or paint to create your designs on the holder.

Make as many pockets as you would like to hold more napkins.

Use the pockets to hold mail.

Pop-Out Puzzle

Young brothers and sisters will get a kick out of playing with this simple puzzle.

You Will Need:

- permanent markers
- plastic-foam tray

1 Draw a simple picture on the flat part of a plastic-foam tray.

2 Carefully cut out the biggest, simplest pieces of your picture from the foam tray without damaging the frame.

3 Fit the cut pieces back into the original picture to solve the puzzle.

More Ideas

Make an *ABC* puzzle for preschoolers.

Foam Frames

Place your favorite face into one of these shapes.

You Will Need:

- large and small plastic-foam trays
- yarn
- photographs or pictures
- paper
- paint and paintbrush
- ribbon
- plastic wrap
- embroidery thread
- large sewing needle

To Make the Yarn Frame

Cut a 3-inch circle from a plastic-foam tray. Cut the center out of the foam circle, leaving a frame about ¾ inch wide. Wrap the frame with yarn. Once your foam frame is completely covered, glue the loose ends of the yarn to the back of the circle. Glue a small picture to the back of the foam circle so the face is peeking through the frame. Add a yarn hanger.

To Make the Bell Frame

Draw and cut out a bell shape from paper. Trace the pattern on a plastic-foam tray and cut it out. Cut a rectangle or other shape in the center to fit your photo. Paint the bell and let dry. Cut a tab from another foam tray. Paint it and let dry. Tape the photo and the tab to the back of the frame. Add ribbon trim.

To Make the Multi-Picture Holder

Cut the sides from two large foam trays. On one piece of foam, cut out circles to fit your photos. Glue a piece of plastic wrap to cover one side of the tray. Spread glue around each circle and place a picture face-down on the plastic wrap, covering each circle. Glue the second plastic-foam tray on top of the first. With thread and a large needle, sew around the edges. Add a hanger.

More Ideas

Make frames in different shapes.
How about a simple truck or a
flower frame?

Plastic-Foam of Plenty

Hang this cornucopia "sculpture" to celebrate the blessings of the Thanksgiving season.

You Will Need:

- large and small plastic-foam trays
- poster board
- paint and paintbrush
- rickrack

2 Draw and cut out various fruit and vegetable shapes from plastic-foam trays. Paint them and let dry.

3 Glue the shapes at the opening of the cornucopia.

4 Glue a strip of rickrack across the top and bottom of the poster board. Add a hanger to the back.

1 Draw and cut out a cornucopia shape from a large plastic-foam tray. Glue it on a piece of poster board.

More Ideas

Instead of a cornucopia, make the turkey shape on page 8 and glue it to a piece of poster board.

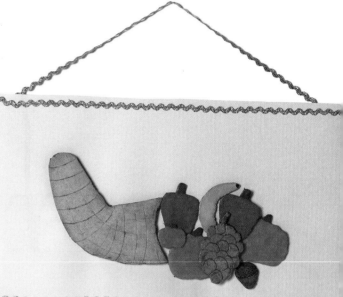

Dresser Tray Keepsake

Your mom or grandmother will treasure this pretty jewelry keeper.

You Will Need:

- large plastic-foam tray
- felt
- ribbon or other trims
- buttons

1 Cut out rectangles from the short sides of a large plastic-foam tray for handles.

2 Cut a piece of felt to fit the bottom of the foam tray and glue in place.

3 Add ribbon or sequins to the curved edges of the tray.

4 Cut felt flowers and glue in place. Add buttons to the center. Let dry.

More Ideas

With marker, write a name on a small rectangular piece of plastic foam, and glue it to the felt bottom to make a nameplate.

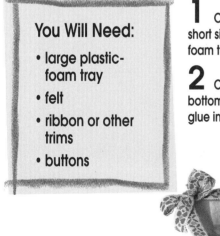

The Book on Foam

Tell your favorite story between these foam covers.

You Will Need:

- large and small plastic-foam trays
- hole punch
- permanent markers
- ribbon
- craft beads
- paper
- large sewing needle
- embroidery thread
- fine-tipped colored pens

To Make the Large Book

Cut the curved edges off two large plastic-foam trays. Write a story and draw pictures on paper that is the same size as the flat foam pieces. Insert the papers between the two pieces of foam. Thread a large needle with embroidery thread and knot the end. Stitch through all layers at the left-hand edge. Decorate the cover with colored pens.

To Make the Tiny Book

Cut the curved edges off two plastic-foam trays. Cut the flat part into four equal "pages." Punch three holes through the pages in exactly the same place. (Punch one page first, then use that page as a pattern for the other three.) Decorate the cover and inside pages with drawings and words about a subject you love. Tie the four pages together at the punched holes with ribbon. Add craft beads through the ends of the ribbon at the bottom.

More Ideas

For a different look, glue colored felt over the front cover, then lace the covers together. Decorate the front with felt cutouts.

Shipshape Sailers

These light-as-a-feather vessels really float.

You Will Need:

- plastic-foam trays
- heavy paper
- markers, construction paper, stickers
- toothpick
- heavy cardboard
- paint and paintbrush
- empty thread spool
- drinking straw

To Make the Sailboard

Cut the bottom of the sailboard from a plastic-foam tray. Cut out the sail from heavy paper. Decorate with markers, construction paper, and other trims. Stick a toothpick mast through the sail, then stick the mast into the board. Add glue to the mast underneath the board so it stays in place.

To Make the Sailboat

Turn a plastic-foam tray upside down on cardboard, and trace around the front part of the tray. Remove the tray, and finish drawing the bow. Cut it out, paint it, and glue it to the top of the tray. Glue an empty thread spool near the bow. Cut a sail from heavy paper, and attach it to a drinking straw for the mast. Insert the mast into the spool.

More Ideas

Add other trims to your boat, such as yarn for a rope or an empty matchbox for a treasure chest.

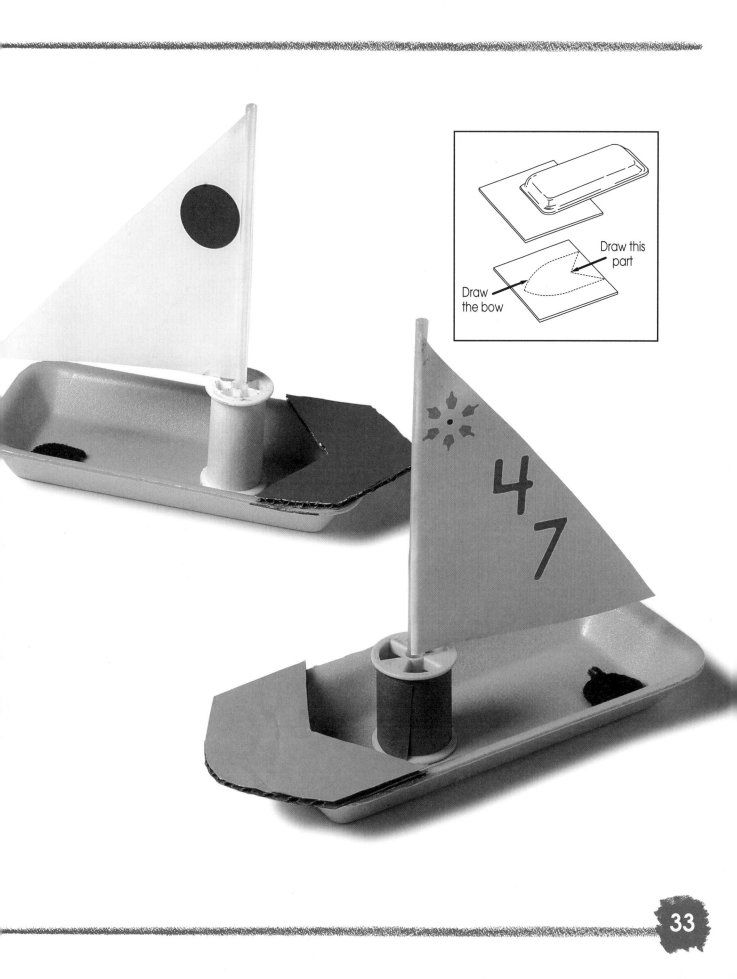

Draw this part

Draw the bow

Stitchery Pictures

With a foam tray and your imagination, you can sew your way to fun.

You Will Need:

- paper
- small plastic-foam trays
- pen or pencil
- large sewing needle
- embroidery thread or yarn

More Ideas

Glue colorful felt to the bottom of your tray before you "poke" your picture into the foam. Then sew.

1 Draw a picture on a piece of paper that is smaller than your plastic-foam tray.

2 Tape the picture to the inside of the tray. With a pen or a pencil, poke holes through the foam tray along the lines of your drawing. Remove the paper.

French knot

straight stitch

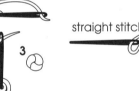

3 With a needle and thread or yarn, sew in and out of the holes using straight stitches or French knots, as shown.

4 Add a thread hanger.

Sukkah Plaque

In the Jewish religion, the Sukkot festival celebrates the harvest of crops and remembers the Israelites who, before they reached the Promised Land, wandered the desert living in temporary shelters, or *sukkahs*.

You Will Need:

- plastic-foam tray
- permanent marker
- fallen twigs
- embroidery thread
- construction paper
- yarn

1 Color the inside of the tray with marker.

2 To make the walls, wrap bunches of twigs with embroidery thread, and glue them around three edges of the plastic-foam tray.

3 Glue on a piece of paper for the floor. Then glue cut-paper fruit, vegetables, and other decorations to the tray.

4 Add a yarn hanger to the back.

More Ideas

Wrap embroidery thread around real straw and glue to the plaque.

Coaster Creations

These foam shapes will keep Mom's table dry.

You Will Need:

- plastic-foam trays
- permanent markers

More Ideas

Make bowl-sized foam circles to protect your table from hot soup bowls.

1 Cut foam shapes that are larger than your drinking glasses.

2 Decorate with markers.

Do-It-Yourself Games

These games are portable and fun to play.

You Will Need:

- plastic-foam trays
- permanent markers
- plastic bag
- ruler
- adhesive Velcro dots

To Make the Tic-Tac-Toe Game

Cut a rectangle from the flat part of a plastic-foam tray. Add tic-tac-toe lines with marker. Cut ten squares from another foam tray. Draw Os on five of the squares and Xs on the other five. Add adhesive Velcro dots to the back of each X and O, and add the Velcro mates to each square on the board.

To Make the Checkers Game

To make the game board, cut the curved sides from a large plastic-foam tray. (The one pictured is about 12 inches by 10¼ inches.) Draw black squares with markers (these are about 1½ inches square), so there is a total of sixty-four squares. To make twenty-four circles, trace around a quarter on foam trays. Color twelve red and twelve black circles. Store your pieces in a plastic bag.

To Make the Match Game

Cut the flat portion of a plastic-foam tray into small squares. Draw the same picture on one side of two squares. Draw a second picture on two more squares. Repeat the process until there are eight pairs.

To play: Lay the squares face-down on a table. Take turns trying to match a picture with its mate.

Store your squares in a plastic bag when you're finished.

More Ideas

For the Match Game, instead of drawing a matching pair, use two identical stickers for each set of squares.

Picket Fence Greeting Magnet

Welcome the new day or new friends with this cheery sign.

You Will Need:

- plastic-foam trays
- magnetic strip
- artificial flowers or cut-paper flowers
- permanent marker

1 Cut six ¾-inch-by-8-inch strips and three ¾-inch-by-6-inch strips from plastic-foam trays.

2 Place the 8-inch strips side by side, with about ¼ inch in between.

3 Glue a 6-inch strip across them, about 1 inch up from the bottom. Glue a second strip about 2 inches down from the top. Add a magnetic strip. Glue the last 6-inch strip diagonally between the first two, forming a Z.

4 Trim the tops to form points.

5 Glue artificial or cut-paper flowers to one side on the front. Write a greeting with marker.

More Ideas

Add a yarn hanger and place the greeting near your front or back door so visitors can see it when they enter your home.

Foam Flutter

This delicate butterfly will light up an indoor plant.

You Will Need:

- permanent markers
- plastic-foam tray
- glitter, sequins, or other trims
- spring-type clothespin
- plastic wiggle eyes
- chenille stick

1 Using markers, draw wing shapes on a plastic-foam tray.

2 Decorate the wings before you cut them out, using markers, glitter, sequins, or other trims.

3 Cut the wings from the foam tray.

4 Glue the wings to the flat side of a spring-type clothespin. Glue two plastic wiggle eyes on top of the other end. Glue on chenille-stick antennae.

5 Attach the flutter to a flowerpot.

More Ideas

Paint a foam tray red and make a ladybug.

Or paint yellow and black stripes for a bee.

Using Your Noodle

Use pasta shapes to create a work of art.

You Will Need:

- uncooked pasta in various shapes and sizes
- plastic-foam tray
- permanent markers

1 Try out designs with different-shaped pasta on a plastic-foam tray.

2 Glue the noodles on the foam tray.

3 After the glue has dried, use markers to draw a background, or leave the background blank.

More Ideas

Choose a foam tray in a color that will complement your picture.

Use colored pasta shapes. Green and orange macaroni are available in grocery stores.

Foam Book Friends

Need a faithful pal to keep track of your book pages? These foam buddies can help.

You Will Need:

- plastic-foam tray
- magazine pictures or gift wrap
- hole punch
- ribbon or embroidery thread

1 Draw a simple shape on the flat surface of a plastic-foam tray.

2 Trace the shape twice on magazine pictures or scraps of gift wrap. Cut them out and glue them to each side of the plastic-foam shape.

3 Use a hole punch to make a hole in the bottom of the shape.

4 Push a loop of ribbon or embroidery thread through the hole, and pull the ends snugly through the loop.

More Ideas

For another kind of bookmark, cut a 6-inch strip of plastic foam, and decorate it with markers or stickers.

Go Foam Fishing

Drop your line in and see what you hook.

You Will Need:

- embroidery thread or string
- 12-inch stick or dowel
- magnet
- plastic-foam trays
- permanent markers
- paper clips

1 Tie thread to the end of the stick.

2 Tie or glue a magnet to the other end of the thread.

3 Draw small fish on a plastic-foam tray. Color them with markers, then cut them out.

4 Poke paper clips through the fish.

To play: "Hook" the fish with the magnet.

More Ideas

Try to get as many fish on the magnet as you can.

Add some other things to catch, such as a treasure chest or a boot.

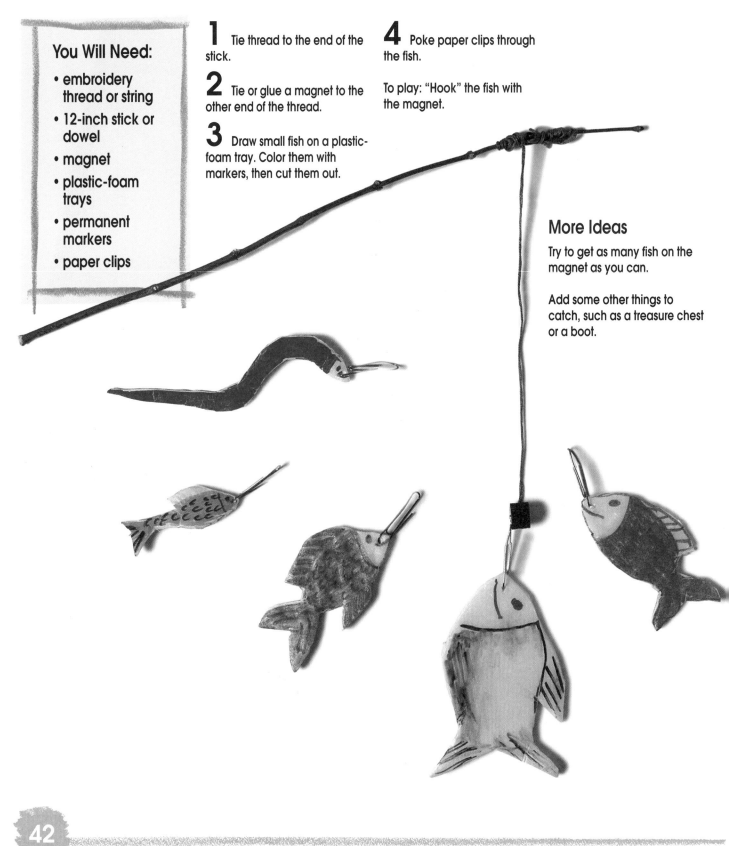

Tri-Star Necklace

Wear this trinket anytime.

You Will Need:

- plastic-foam tray
- permanent markers
- hole punch
- satin ribbon

1 On the flat part of a plastic-foam tray, draw three star shapes and cut them out.

2 Color both sides of the shapes. Decorate if you wish.

3 Punch a hole in each star at the top.

4 Tie a tiny loop of satin ribbon through the holes. Cut an 18-inch length of ribbon. Hang the stars from the ribbon. Knot the ends.

More Ideas

Make a moon to add to your outer-space theme.

Try some leaves or flowers to hang on your necklace.

Add smaller shapes to a shorter length of ribbon to create a bracelet.

Work-of-Art Frame

Display your favorite personal drawings.

You Will Need:

- paper
- plastic-foam tray
- markers or crayons
- satin ribbon
- sequins

1 Cut paper to fit inside a plastic-foam tray.

2 Draw a picture on the paper with markers or crayons.

3 Glue the picture to the flat part of the tray.

4 Add a border of satin ribbon around the picture. Decorate the curved sides of the tray with sequins. Add a ribbon hanger to the top.

More Ideas

Glue rickrack around the edge of the tray.

Use a colored plastic-foam tray instead of white.

Cast of Stand-Up Characters

Invite these creatures to your next Halloween party.

To Make the Basic Character

1 Draw a shape on a plastic-foam tray and cut it out.

2 Cut two notches at the bottom of your character.

3 Cut a circle from a foam tray, then cut it in half.

4 Slide the half circles into the notches.

To Make the Pumpkin

Color your pumpkin shape. Add dark lines down the shape to add dimension.

To Make the Cat

Draw features and legs with colored chalk. Add a collar of glitter.

To Make the Ghosts

Draw features with marker. Outline the ghost in black marker if you wish. Add a pumpkin made of plastic foam or construction paper. Decorate, then glue on a paper or ribbon handle.

To Make the Witch

Add features with paint, and create a glittering gown and hat.

More Ideas

Cut out dolls or other figures. To make clothes, trace the figures on paper, adding tabs. Decorate the clothes and cut them out.

You can make shapes for other occasions. How about a turkey for Thanksgiving? Or try a likeness of yourself on your birthday.

Fabric and Foam Birdhouse

Bird watchers will love this special wall hanging.

You Will Need:

- large plastic-foam trays
- fabric
- lace or other fabric trims
- construction paper
- artificial flower
- yarn

1 Draw a house shape and a roof shape on plastic-foam trays. Cut them out.

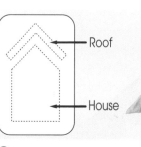

Roof

House

2 Wrap fabric over the house and the roof, taping the fabric to the back. Glue the roof to the house.

3 Add fabric trim, such as lace, to the roof.

4 Cut and glue on pieces of construction paper for the bird, door, and stem.

5 Add an artificial flower at the top of the stem. Glue a yarn hanger to the back.

More Ideas

Foam makes a sturdy base for wall hangings. Make a basket shape from plastic foam and cover it with spring-type fabric for an easy Easter display.

Hands Around the Clock

Help your younger siblings learn to tell time.

You Will Need:

- large plastic-foam tray
- number stickers
- cardboard
- marker
- metal paper fastener

1 Cut a circle from a plastic-foam tray.

2 Add number stickers on the clock.

3 Cut the hands from cardboard. Color them with marker.

4 Push a metal paper fastener through both hands and through the center of the clock.

More Ideas

Decorate your clock to make it your own. Add pictures or glitter.

Set the clock to remind you of an important time, such as the hour when soccer practice begins.

Just "Plane" Fun

Get ready for takeoff.

You Will Need:

- paper
- large plastic-foam tray
- permanent markers, stickers
- paper clip

1 On paper, draw a pattern for the airplane parts as shown and cut them out.

2 Trace around the patterns on a plastic-foam tray. Cut out the pieces.

3 Add details with markers, stickers, or anything else you can think of.

4 Slip a paper clip on the nose of your plane to help it fly better.

More Ideas

Use the walls of the castle on page 26 to make an airplane hangar.

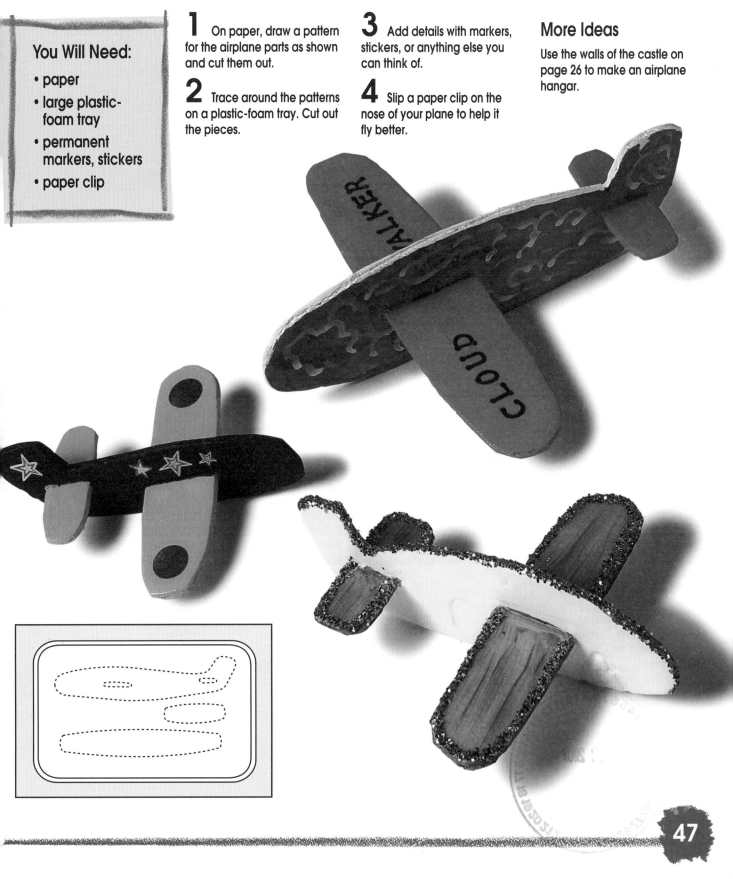

Title Index

Animal Foam Faces 20
Beads and Bangles Jewelry . . 18
Bits-and-Pieces Mosaic 14
Book on Foam, The 31
Cast of Stand-Up Characters . 44
Christmas Cutouts 12
Coaster Creations 35
Coupon Catcher 14
Cut-It-Up Puzzle 6
Do-It-Yourself Games 36
Dresser Tray Keepsake 30
Fabric and Foam Birdhouse . . 46
Festive Foam Hang-Ups 24
Foam Book Friends 40
Foam-Disk Wigglers 10
Foam-Fish Bowl 6
Foam Flutter 38
Foam Frames 28
Garden Markers 22
Go Foam Fishing 42
Greetings for the Seasons 8
Hands Around the Clock 46
Just "Plane" Fun 47
Little Chicken 11
Medieval Castle 26
Mobile Magic 16
My Bulletin Board 4
Napkin Pocket 27
Nest of Chicks 22
Nifty Nameplates 11
Picket Fence Greeting Magnet . 38
Plastic-Foam of Plenty 30
Pop-Out Puzzle 27
Shield of Honor 1
Shipshape Sailers 3
Something's Fishy Aquarium . . 1
Stained-Glass Tissue Window . 2
Stitchery Pictures 3
Sukkah Plaque 3
Tabletop Weather Vanes . . . . . .
Tri-Star Necklace 4
Using Your Noodle 3
Wacky Masks 1
Work-of-Art Frame 4

Subject Index

ANIMALS
Animal Foam Faces 20, 21
Ant 10
Bear 20
Bee 10
Bird mobile 17
Butterfly mobile 17
Cast of Stand-Up
  Characters 44, 45
Cat 20, 44
Cat mask 15
Fabric and Foam Birdhouse . . 46
Foam-Disk Wigglers 10
Foam-Fish Bowl 6
Foam Flutter 38
Go Foam Fishing 42
Lion 20
Little Chicken 11
Monkey 20
Nest of Chicks 22
Rabbit 21
Something's Fishy Aquarium . . 19
Tabletop Weather Vanes 7
Worm 10

CONTAINERS
Coupon Catcher 14
Napkin Pocket 27

GAMES
Checkers game 36
Do-It-Yourself Games 36, 37
Go Foam Fishing 42
Hands Around the Clock 46
Match game 36
Tic-Tac-Toe game 36

GIFTS
Bell frame 28
Christmas card 9
Coaster Creations 35
Dresser Tray Keepsake 30
Foam Book Friends 40, 41
Foam Frames 28, 29
Greetings for the Seasons . . . 8, 9
Hanukkah card 9
Multi-picture holder 28
Thanksgiving card 8
Valentine's Day card 8
Yarn frame 28
Yom Kippur card 9

HOLIDAY AND OTHER
  DECORATIONS
Animal Foam Faces 20, 21
Bear 20
Bird mobile 17
Bits-and-Pieces Mosaic 14
Butterfly mobile 17
Cast of Stand-Up
  Characters 44, 45
Cat 20, 44
Christmas Cutouts 12, 13
Easter egg 24
Fabric and Foam Birdhouse . . 46
Fabric board 5
Fabric-squares board 5
Festive Foam Hang-Ups . . 24, 25
Flag 25
Foam-Fish Bowl 6
Foam Flutter 38
Ghost 24
Ghosts 44

GIFTS (continued)
Lion 20
Little Chicken 11
Memo board 4
Mini bulletin board 4
Mobile Magic 16, 17
Monkey 20
My Bulletin Board 4, 5
Napkin Pocket 27
Nest of Chicks 22
Nifty Nameplates 11
Picket Fence Greeting
  Magnet 38
Plastic-Foam of Plenty 30
Pumpkin 44
Rabbit 21
Shamrock mobile 16
Shield of Honor 19
Something's Fishy Aquarium . . 19
Stained-Glass Tissue Window . 23
Star of David 25
Stitchery Pictures 34
Sukkah Plaque 35
Sunshine mobile 16
Tabletop Weather Vanes 7
Using Your Noodle 39
Valentine's Day heart 24
Witch 44
Work-of-Art Frame 43

PLANT ACCESSORIES
Foam Flutter 38
Garden Markers 22

THINGS TO WEAR
Beads and Bangles
  Jewelry 18
Bracelets 18
Heart necklace 18
Tri-Star Necklace 4

TOYS
Ant 10
Bee 10
Book on Foam, The 31
Cat mask 15
Clown mask 15
Cut-It-Up Puzzle 6
Foam-Disk Wigglers 10
Just "Plane" Fun 47
Large book 31
Medieval Castle 26
Pop-Out Puzzle 27
Sailboard 33
Sailboat 33
Shipshape Sailers 32, 33
Snow mask 15
Tiny book 31
Wacky Masks 15
Worm 10

VESSELS AND VEHICLES
Just "Plane" Fun 47
Sailboard 33
Sailboat 33
Shipshape Sailers 32, 33